Mary at age 121 in Chattanooga.

Mary reads to her teacher, Helen Kelley.

Helen Kelley presents Mary with her first graduation certificate, which declares that she can read.

To my big sister, Marlena D. Russell, who loved to share
her first-grade vocabulary words with me —R.L.H.

To my mentors, April and Judy-Sue —O.M.

Text copyright © 2020 by Rita Lorraine Hubbard
Jacket art and interior illustrations copyright © 2020 by Oge Mora

All rights reserved. Published in the United States by Schwartz & Wade Books, an imprint of
Random House Children's Books, a division of Penguin Random House LLC, New York.
Schwartz & Wade Books and the colophon are trademarks of Penguin Random House LLC.

Visit us on the Web! rhcbooks.com
Educators and librarians, for a variety of teaching tools, visit us at RHTeachersLibrarians.com

Library of Congress Cataloging-in-Publication Data
Names: Hubbard, Rita L., author. | Mora, Oge, illustrator.
Title: The oldest student: how Mary Walker learned to read / Rita Lorraine
Hubbard; [illustrated by] Oge Mora.
Description: First edition. | New York City: Schwartz & Wade Books, [2020] | Audience: Ages: 4–8.
Audience: Grades: K–3. Identifiers: LCCN 2019007529 | ISBN 978-1-5247-6828-7 (hardcover)
ISBN 978-1-5247-6829-4 (hardcover library binding) | ISBN 978-1-5247-6830-0 (ebook)
Subjects: LCSH: Walker, Mary, 1848–1969—Juvenile literature. | Women slaves—United States—Biography—Juvenile literature.
Freedmen—United States—Biography—Juvenile literature. | Illiterate persons—United States—Biography—Juvenile literature.
Classification: LCC E444 .W235 H83 2020 | DDC 306.3/62092 [B]—dc23

The text of this book is set in Adobe Caslon.
The illustrations were rendered in acrylic paint, china marker, colored pencil, patterned paper, and book clippings.
Book design by Rachael Cole

MANUFACTURED IN CHINA
2 4 6 8 10 9 7 5 3 1
First Edition

SELECTED BIBLIOGRAPHY

Bowles, Jay. "Former Slave Is Nation's Oldest Student." *Modern Maturity.* Feb–Mar, 1967: 27.

Collins, J. B. "Ex-Slave Says First Airplane Ride 'No Different from Hoss and Buggy.'" *News Free Press.* May 6, 1966.

Edwards, Jr., John Loyd. *The Ex-Slave Extra: Never Too Old, Coming from Slavery thru Slums to Celebrity.* Help, Inc., 1976.

"'Grandma' Walker's Inspiration." *Chattanooga Post.* December 4, 1969.

Gunn, T. R. "A Slave Who Escaped." *Mahogany.* July 24, 1979: 17.

"Literacy Student, Age 99, Honored on Birthday." *Chattanooga Times.* June 2, 1965. [Historical Note: It has been determined that
    Mary Walker was 116 years old on June 2, 1965.]

Ozmer, Marianne. "103 and Still Going Strong." *News Free Press.* May 7, 1969. [Historical Note: It has been determined that
    Mary Walker was 121 years of age in 1969.]

Patten, Lee. "Gramma Honored on 100th Birthday." *Chattanooga Times.* May 7, 1966. [Historical Note: It has been determined that
    Mary Walker was 117 years old on this date.]

THE OLDEST STUDENT

HOW MARY WALKER LEARNED TO READ

WRITTEN BY

RITA LORRAINE HUBBARD

ILLUSTRATED BY

OGE MORA

schwartz & wade books · new york

Whenever young Mary Walker was tired, she would shield her eyes from the sun and watch the swallow-tailed kites dip and soar above the trees.

That must be what it's like to be free, she thought.

But Mary didn't watch for long. Even at only eight years old, she knew the first rule of the Union Springs, Alabama, plantation she lived on:

KEEP WORKING!

She knew the second rule, too: slaves should not be taught to read or write, or do anything that might help them learn to do so.

Mary didn't stop working. She didn't learn to read, either. But at the end of each long day picking cotton, toting water to Papa and the other slaves who chopped wood for the train tracks, or helping Mama clean the Big House, she would lie in her little bed next to the crumbling fireplace and think about those birds.

When I'm free, I'll go where I want and rest when I want. And I'll learn to read, too.

When she was fifteen, it happened. Mary and her mother, brothers, and sister were free; the Emancipation Proclamation said so. What it didn't say was how a family with nothing except the tattered garments on their backs could find food, clothes, and a place to sleep. Mary's father had died, and the family was on its own.

FREEDOM ROAD!
TO FREEDOM ROAD!

Across fields and through woods, ex-slaves
surged like waves crashing hard to shore. (Now
that they were free, every road was Freedom Road.)
Many headed north and west and every which way,
searching for long-lost family members, or simply
experiencing the wonder of being free.

Others, like Mary, chose to stay in the South. An organization called the Freedmen's Bureau helped those who stayed to find shelter on abandoned Confederate land. Mary and her family settled in a one-room cabin, and for the next few years, she worked alongside her mama to help feed her siblings. Seven days a week she churned butter, cleaned houses, and cared for other folks' children.

The hours were long, and if Mary was thirsty or hungry or needed to use the outhouse, she had to wait until she got home. At week's end, she would offer Mama the one lonely quarter she had earned.

One day Mary met a group of evangelists on the roadside.
A woman with soft wrinkles in her kindly face placed a big,
beautiful Bible in Mary's hands, and told her,

YOUR CIVIL RIGHTS ARE
IN THESE PAGES

Mary didn't know what civil rights were. She only knew that
top to bottom, front to back, that book was filled with words.
I'm going to learn to read those words, she vowed.
But not today. Today there was work to be done.

And tomorrow, too.

When Mary got married, she and her husband worked as sharecroppers—renting someone else's house, using someone else's tools, and planting someone else's seeds to farm land they would never own.

After they harvested the crops, almost all the money they earned went to pay for the housing, tool, and seed costs.

Mary was twenty years old when her first son was born.

She opened her Bible and marveled at the squiggles inside. There had been no time to learn to read.

A friend wrote Mary's son's birth date in the Bible: August 26, 1869.

Then Mary dipped a pen into an inkwell and made her mark beside it.

Not a letter, not a name, just a mark. It was the best she could do.

One day Mary's husband died. She married again, and a second son was born. Then a third. Mary made marks for these sons, too. Now she had three growing boys.

More money, that's what we need, Mary thought.

But the only other jobs available to black women were as maids or nannies or cooks. The hours were long, with only half a day off on Saturdays, and like sharecropping, they didn't pay much.

Mary sighed. Words would have to wait.

For the next four decades, Mary sharecropped and did odd jobs to help support her family.

In 1917, Mary's family moved to the little city of Chattanooga, Tennessee. It was the year of Chattanooga's Great Flood. The story was in all the newspapers, but Mary could only study the pictures to understand what had happened.

By now Mary was sixty-eight and too old to sharecrop, but she continued to work, cooking, cleaning, and babysitting. She also fried fish, baked cakes, and sold sandwiches to raise money for her church.

On Sundays she would sit in the congregation, and as the preacher spoke,
she would clutch her family Bible—the Bible she still couldn't read.

When Mary was well past ninety, she and her husband sat in their creaky rockers while one or another of their sons read to them. After the two younger boys died, the eldest read. Then Mary's husband died. Several years later, her eldest son died, too. He was ninety-four.

Mary had outlived her entire family. She was 114 years old and alone.

"Can't read," she said. "Can't write. I don't know anything."

Mary stood at the window of her retirement home and gazed down at the world below. Words were everywhere: on billboards, on buildings, on store windows and trucks.

She sighed. *All this time*, she thought, *and they still look like squiggles.*

Mary had heard about a new reading class held in her building.

She pursed her lips. "No more waiting," she decided. "Time to learn."

Out of her apartment, into an elevator, and down to the lobby she went.
When the elevator doors sprang open, Mary saw people sitting under a sign
with a picture of an open book. She could not read the words.

A neighbor walked up to her. "That's a reading class, Miss Mary.
Can I help you over?"

Mary shook her head. Then she gripped her cane, lifted her chin,
and walked straight toward that sign.

For the next year and more, Mary put everything she had into learning to read. It wasn't easy; after all, she was the oldest student in the class—and probably in the entire country. Could someone her age learn to read? She didn't know, but by God, she was going to try.

She studied the alphabet until her eyes watered. She memorized the sounds each letter made and practiced writing her name so many times that her fingers cramped. She learned to recognize "sight words" and then challenged herself to make short sentences with them.

She studied and studied, until books and pages and letters and words swirled in her head while she slept.

One fine day Mary's hard work paid off. She could read!
Word of her accomplishment traveled, and people
everywhere celebrated with her. Chattanooga's mayor,
newspaper journalists across the country, and a man from
the US Department of Education, who said, "Mrs. Mary
Walker, I pronounce you the nation's oldest student,"
all shared her joy.

HAPPY
BIRTHDAY,
GRAMMA
WALKER

BUY

STOP

THE TOWERS

BAKERY

PUB

Mary felt complete. She still missed her sons, but whenever she was lonely, she read from her Bible or looked out her window and read the words in the street below.

From then on, Chattanoogans honored Mary's achievement with yearly birthday parties. In 1966, President Lyndon B. Johnson sent well wishes on Mary's 118th birthday, and in 1969, President Richard Nixon did the same. Mary was now 121 years old.

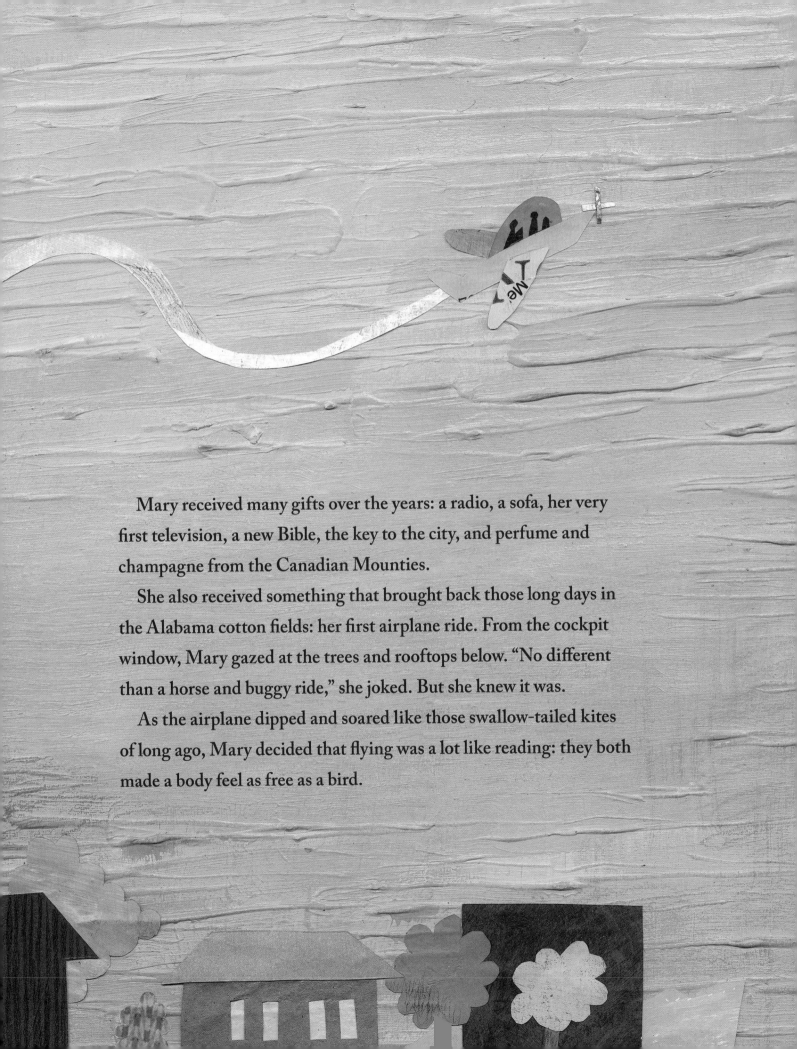

Mary received many gifts over the years: a radio, a sofa, her very first television, a new Bible, the key to the city, and perfume and champagne from the Canadian Mounties.

She also received something that brought back those long days in the Alabama cotton fields: her first airplane ride. From the cockpit window, Mary gazed at the trees and rooftops below. "No different than a horse and buggy ride," she joked. But she knew it was.

As the airplane dipped and soared like those swallow-tailed kites of long ago, Mary decided that flying was a lot like reading: they both made a body feel as free as a bird.

Each year, before her birthday celebration came to an end, someone would whisper, "Let's listen to Miss Mary." The shuffling and movement would fade away until not a sound was heard.

Then Mary would stand on her old, old legs, clear her old, old throat, and read from her Bible or her schoolbook in a voice that was clear and strong.

When she finished, she would gently close her
book and say,

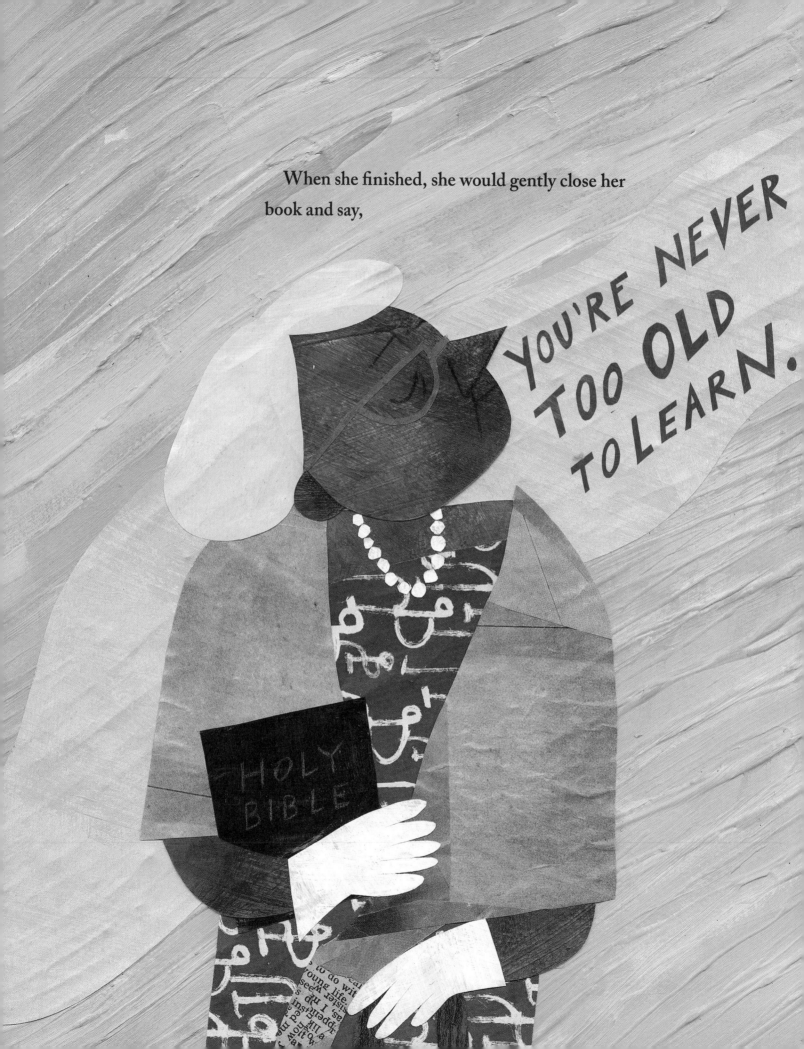

YOU'RE NEVER
TOO OLD
TO LEARN.

HOLY
BIBLE

AUTHOR'S NOTE

Mary Walker was born a slave on May 6, 1848. From a young age, she picked cotton, toted water, cleaned houses, and worked as a blacksmith. In later life, she never forgot the harsh punishments slaves received if they stopped working without permission, but she was quick to say that she had forgiven everyone for the things she'd endured.

Very little is known about Mary's life from her emancipation at age fifteen until she learned to read at 116, but it is a fact that her Bible waited 101 years for her to learn to read it! It is known that Mary was married twice and had three sons. One of those sons served in World War I.

I chose to imagine other details to fill in the blanks.

Mary's eldest son died in 1963. She enrolled in CALM, the Chattanooga Area Literacy Movement, the same year, and by 1964, she knew how to read, write, add, and subtract. She was then certified as the nation's oldest student and was twice named Chattanooga's Ambassador of Goodwill. Her retirement home was renamed the Mary Walker Towers.

Mary received the key to the city of Chattanooga in 1966 and 1969. Her first airplane ride happened on May 6, 1966, when pilot Harry Porter flew her over her apartment building so she could wave to her friends below.

Before Mary's death at age 121 on December 1, 1969, she could still see and hear well. She could still hold a pencil and write her name steadily, and she could walk with only minimal help from her trusty cane. She could also still sew beautiful bonnets, and bake cakes that she bragged were "light as a feather."

Mary lived through twenty-six presidents. Today Historical Marker 2A73 stands at 3031 Wilcox Boulevard in Chattanooga, Tennessee, to commemorate her amazing life.

Mary reads her favorite book, the Bible.

Mary's first airplane ride.

Mary being feted on her 99th birthday.